Life's Journey of Healing Poetry

Gary Nielsen

BookLeaf
Publishing

Presentation by *BookLeaf Publishing*

Web: www.bookleafpub.com

E-mail: info@bookleafpub.com

ISBN: 9789357748568

First edition 2023

*I would like to dedicate this book to
everybody that had a helping hand in my
recovery,*

my two sons: "Trey","Charlie"

My family

ACKNOWLEDGEMENT

This wouldn't be possible without the treatment centers out there that helped save my life. Cedar Ridge, Oak Ridge, Burkwood, and Lakeshore. Just a couple of the important treatment facilities I personally attended and give credit to for my still being here to release this book.

I also wanted to dedicate this book to those out there still suffering that feel so alone. You are not alone, there are many of us out there, keep fighting, you are worth it!

PREFACE

Feeling alone? Have a seat, pick a title and start to relate. In the self-help book coming to you from a first-hand experience, something to relate to, and learn from! Enjoy this new author, sharing with you personal experience on the journey through life, battling addiction, turmoil, death, happiness, anxiety, and legal trouble. This is to encourage, enlighten, educate, support, and to help spread the support to all of those still suffering!

Lending Hand

The Everlasting battle,
between Jesus and myself,
my right hand holding the answer,
what the backup on the Shelf,
I slowly insert the relief,
but for some reason I can't feel,
the world disappears around me,
this just doesn't seem real,
With smoke in my eyes,
and the liquor changing lanes,
to make way for the Venom,
that I'm putting in my veins,
can't wait to be happy, feel good,
and be in charge,
with more gambling in front of me,
It's either slots or playing cards,
but again what is this delay,
why is it I can't feel,
the relief I'm used to grabbing,
there's just something surreal,
that's happening to me now,
it's not my arm that I see,
are my eyes playing tricks on me,
truly can this be,
when my left ear captures,

a voice so soft and smooth,
no longer are you needing this,
along with all the booze,
the gambling that is out,
and family steps back in,
through the door to your back,
with fresh oil on the hinge,
that creaked so loud every time,
you stepped into this room,
and place yourself in these four walls,
and they slowly did consume,
our lives in an instance,
and put make-believe In our eyes,
so when they see the light,
what they see are the Devil's lies,
but the last time that door opened,
it was Jesus that came in,
He said it's time to clean the house,
and get rid of all the sins,
And slowly start to capture,
my reflection in the mirror,
look at it with confidence,
see beauty and persevere,
through these times of toughness,
and step into the light,
surrounded by family and friends,
each and every night,
so let this be a lesson,
of what Christ can do for us,

his lending hand is more than that,
It's the one that we can trust!
2 / 3

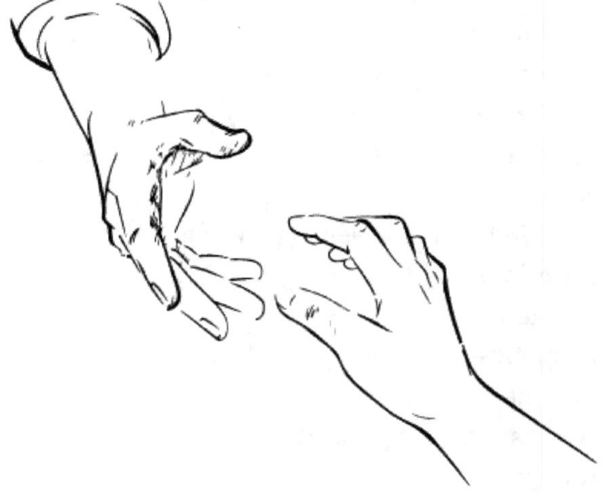

Lord's Bandaid

Conceited like the devil, with ears locked up
tight,
demons flock around me, it seems there is no
right,
place in this world, for my beauty to shine
through,
my bleeding heart trickles down, and reveals just
how blue,
the weight truly is, I constantly look back,
to where I turned wrong, wishing I was on track,
but it slowly seeps back in, these methods that
will pull,
my mind to the present, and teach me to let go,
learn from my footprints, that stagger right
behind me,
let my lesson settle in, and the results come and
find the,
Angels with footprints, that seem so hard to
follow,
and slowly patch this heart, that used to dread
tomorrow,
now no longer do I hide, the blood stain on my
shirt,
and my heart beats so strong, because the Lord's
bandaids work.

An Unknown Journey

If I had to guess, when I was a child,
where my life would lead, it sure is wild,
It would come in chapters, one after another,
this live Angel asking, for guidance from his
mother,
through this life, of ups and downs,
every corner I turn, it is this that I found,
It was different indeed, it was not what I
expected,
these things in life, that I've slowly collected,
many lessons learned, brought me to understand,
there sure is a reason, I'm here on this land,
that only a dream, it was once before,
I was just praying to God, please give me some
more,
strength and hope, because it seems to be fading,
but now the doubt and worry, I can see myself
trading,
for happiness and joy, that fell in my heart,
I'm so excited for, the next chapter to start,
so different from the last, it's like a new
beginning,
my soul now cleansed, I surely seem to be
winning,
sharing my story, to inspire all the weak,

Encouraging everyone, to their story to speak,
to push on and pray, away all the worry,
because we all are alike, on an unknown
Journey!

Thankful for Clouds

With memories up in smoke, they fill the sky with clouds, from all the sins we have committed, and things we have allowed, as long as there's a breath in me, I will beat the devil down, fight him off with the lord, because my heart won't be around, Satan or addiction, because one uses the other, to steer us in his direction, like trying to change the weather, well this weather won't be changed, because I am my own storm, my soul repaired and pieced together, my heart no longer torn, in-between sin and pain, no more, thanks, to the Lord, who kept me on the safe path, but provided me the sword, to fight off the devil, because my life is a story, that's already been written, and now I show my glory, the shine in my halo, and the width of my wings, as I sail to new heights, and achieve amazing things, I'm so thankful for Jesus, and all that he allows, especially for sobriety, and us for providing clouds.

Rise Again

Another day of living, with no high-speed crash, focused on the future, and reflecting on the past, live every day in beauty, and let the sunshine in, and thank the Lord above, for removing all the sin, support from our brothers, our family and our friends, and pride for myself, for letting Christ to step in, wear that badge of honor, and motivate the shaky, giving thanks for resurrection, while enjoying this here gravy, life left to live, not just topping for this supper, the most beautiful thing I've heard, is the cross he hung to suffer, to forgive our sinful ways, so we can love in peace, what a wonderful day it is, knowing there's relief, and a purpose for my life, in my heart, and in my future, no matter how deep the wound, Christ always has a suitor, to stop a bleeding heart, and to even out the beat, because even Jesus himself, rose back onto his feet.

You And I

With new thoughts in mind, and a future that's so bright, all I can think about, is holding you so tight, something that has never, been tempted yet before, so just that in itself, says it's worth it to explore, regardless of what the past, has shown for you and I, it seems that the limit, is nothing but the sky, so who is to say, that this cannot be true, when all I can think about, it's just me and you, on a New path, well actually it's the same, but now have these tools, that God gave us to shame, addiction, yes the devil, himself will run in fear, and no longer will you rest, having shed a tear, so when you lay down to sleep, remember you are loved, especially by your children, and the man that's up above, because people truly care, for you I cannot lie, so brace yourself for the future, when it's just you and I.

Meant to Be

When it's meant to be, through hell and high water, our love will survive, it is mended by our father, up so high above us, he is keeping our hearts, safe from day one, there was no falling apart, you being my queen, and I being your king, there's no number of years, that could step in between, our love that is pure, as a raging river flowing, he gave us reassurance, and kept the both of us knowing, that we were meant to be, and that he did have a plan, knowing where we would pull through, and proudly make a stand, so very tall and so proud, showing everybody it's possible, to prevent the devil from intruding, and strengthening love to colossal, measures indeed, nobody will argue that, with strong feelings in between us, it's time to make some tracks, in the next chapter of life, just me holding on to you, when I said it's meant to be, I was telling you the truth.

Blessed Behavior

With a new way of life, and veins all cleared, of traffic jam toxins, finally disappeared, sober community surrounds, next chapter begins, eating, breathing, loving you, no more having to sin, to feel in control, to be someone in life, I proudly hold my head, high and think twice, when temptation appears, and the devil starts dancing, around me and laughing, thinking I'm relapsing, when my shield shines bright, and the Lord's sword comes down, the devil falls being defeated, and runs with a frown, a warrior at heart, and cupid's hole to love, precious Angels surround, so beautiful like a dove, singing and floating, with a life of no worry, freedom is granted, and life is not blurry, but clear as a spring, water fed pool, we swim in the blessings, baptized and retooled, for bright futures and love, and Christ as our savior, I thank him everyday for this blessed new behavior.

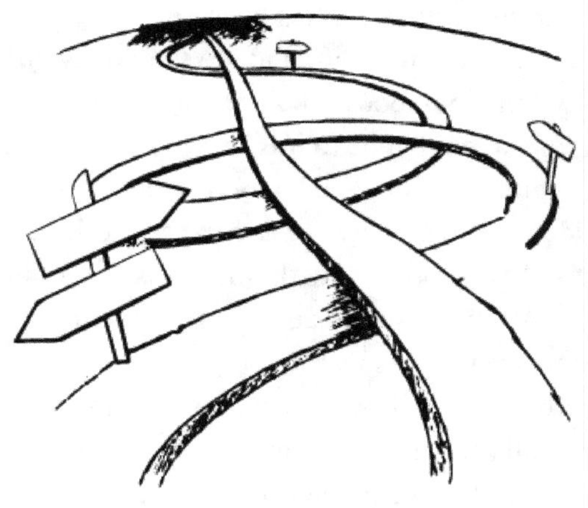

Invisible Road

Suddenly there's a crash, there I lay upside down, what could possibly have happened, I didn't even hear a sound, in such a short moment, my whole life has been changed, what possibly could have I hit, and are they okay, did I really hurt somebody, and are they on their way, to heaven thanks to me, driving like a fool, who decided I didn't need, any of God's tools, he provided me to fix, the vehicle we called life, because I was too ashamed, mine wasn't running right, now hearts surely ache, not for them but for me, because this was no accident, with anybody you see, I was on the road of life, just like we all are, just trying to get somewhere, not particularly far, the place is called happiness, with my family and my friends, when I get to this place, is where the road ends, well let me tell you loved ones, it can be a heavy load, but with God and his trailer, we Will conquer The invisible Road.

Love Rich

When I'm laid down to rest, love rich I will be, my heart completely filled, and my soul so healthy, with a new chapter to come, materials I will not take, because in this life, there's only so much you can make, but rest assured you cannot, take it with you when you go, no matter how you ask, he will still tell you no, love is all I accept, to bring with you when you come, something I've been giving you, since you were born on day one, so please bring it all, and hold it dearly in your heart, it's something I've been telling you, since the very start, whether or not you were listening, that was up to you, but one thing is for certain, you and I are never through, so hold your head high, this separation will be brief, your family understand angel, sit back and let them grieve, remember what you're holding, so deep inside your heart, purer than all money, you've been loved rich from the start.

When Angels Visit

When Angels visit, who do they see, do they
visit other angels, are they people like me, are
their wings like a dove, with halos of gold, or do
they all look different, with their story untold, so
how will I know, when an angel visits me, will
someone say hey, it's your turn to see, well how
did you know, if that's how it goes, did your
heart fill with joy, was your story now told, well
it was Jesus you see, who grabbed me by the
hand, and said let me take you, to a very special
land, the land of serenity, were blankets are
made up of love, the clouds are made of pillows,
you now feel you are above, addiction and all
sorrow, no longer control me, now it's so simple,
in the mirror the Angels me.

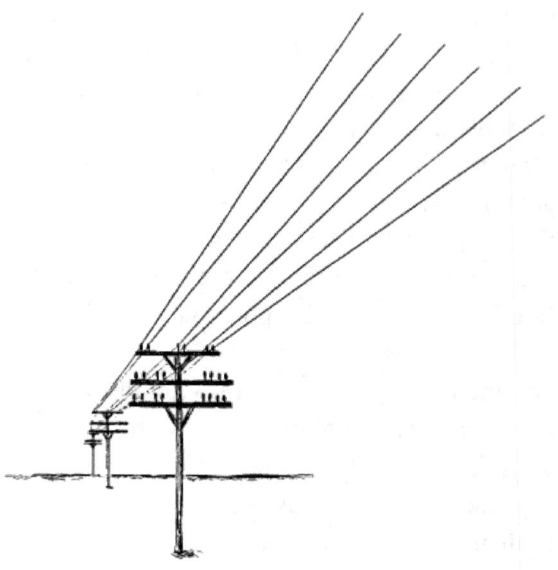

Unarmed

How can one be so dangerous, forever unarmed,
what could I possibly do, to cause someone
harm, it's not what we do, but the energy we put
off, that others do feel, and pay the real cost,
what is the cost we give, we call it real pain, so
often love the ones feel, the bleeding from our
gain, but try to reach out, they try to lend a hand,
they try to pick us up, and take us to the land,
the land is called serenity, where love is thick
like fog, it totally falls upon you, like a love
happy dog, always happy to see you, and never
holding a grudge, Jesus our savior, the one and
only real judge, how lucky can we be,
considering he forgives, never convicting a
sentence, where nobody wants to live, just hope
faith and love, to carry us on our way, now
surely I am armed, with his love here to stay.

Above the Weather

Your mind and heart, shine true as ever, whoever created it, boy they were clever, with peace in mind, and a future so bright, his love is sure, to keep you warm at night, with tears all shed, them days are all over, no more sinful ways, and no more hangovers, they are days of the past, but not to be ashamed, because life is a lesson, and some can't be tamed, but the journey is real, and struggle even stronger, and it will make you want to quit, and not try any longer, but our hearts that bleed, can be patched by a man, even though a carpenter, he built us to withstand, the worst of the worst, or so we thought, but he hung on the cross, it was our sins he brought, with him when he died, so we could all go, peaceful to heaven, past the clouds and the snow.

Unanswered Request

What should I do, what do you suggest, how
should I react to these unanswered requests,
does this mean no love, does this mean Bridges
burned, or should I chalk it up, as another lesson
learned, should I be upset, or should it be
expected, from the life I chose, this is what is
reflected, from my actions in the past, I guess it's
no surprise, so I will take it in stride, sit back
and realize, one person I can turn to, the Lord up
above, or any kind of answer, he'll fill my heart
with love, all I have to do, is open up my eyes,
and look for his signs, he doesn't tell no lies,
recognize his lending hand, when he's reaching
out for me, to pick me up and dust me off, and
continue with my story, of how I fought every
battle, with him we're the best, because not
much did he, leave me an unanswered request.

A Guardian Within Me

A guardian within me, is there such a thing, does
this mean two people, or is it like a spring,
springing into protect, such very vital things,
like all important organs, or is it fictional you
see, what we try to save, truly it can be, a very
tough task, trying to keep it safe, try to keep it
from escaping, trying to get away, God's love is
what I speak of, I'm trying to hold dear, keep it
deep in my heart, and hold it very near, share but
not give away, because all of us need, his love to
help us heal, these aching hearts that bleed.

Sentenced To Life

Life is a sentence, the outcome is our choice, we can look in the mirror, sit back and rejoice, or sit back sit down, and really do ponder, why does life lead me, to constantly wander, what is it I need, in this called life, what is it I want, why do I think twice, when doing the right thing, it seems I study, things too hard, when He is right above me, always watching me, and decisions that I make, with some of the outcomes, He watches life take, away precious time, I surely will miss, but still He watches me, constantly dismiss, these things that do not, sink in until here, it seems locked abroad, but still very near, loved ones who matter, and places of concerned, I just need to take note, and that I can learn, right from wrong, and wrong from right, if we believe in Jesus, He will show us the light

Decisions

Decisions I must make, slowly start to take, over in my mind, and I start to think great, things can be possible, achievement can be had, don't let the fear be there, don't let the lesson grab, me unexpectedly, and shy you far away, let the lesson learned, be planted there to stay, fresh in my mind, and reminded here and there, of what it cost to get, the lesson that lands me fair and square, in this single colored outfit, and asking to bounce a ball, and permission needed in itself, just to walk the hall, it all adds up to, things we must learn, like all of our actions, that could put us in an urn, how to stay alive, how to stay real happy, that's right about the time, I feel Jesus grab me, with this hammer in one hand, and tape in the other, He said I'm not just a carpenter, that builds a solid structure, but molding people's futures, when they pray and ask, is something I do enjoy, out of many tasks, so pray to me young angel, whenever your heart's in doubt, and answers will come to you, and no longer you will pout.

Don't Panic

Don't panic take a breath, and let the light show you, how bright a day can be, like a brand new tattoo, forever in our life, like the ink it's here to stay, to guide us and love us, and to see us all the way, back to His Kingdom, with a lifetime of memories, from childhood to running wild, all the way to recovery, a proud angel we shall stand, having learned the most, from our paths by choice, that made us feel like ghost, but Christ goes all in, and deep into her hearts, to be the glue we all need, to piece together broken parts, so don't panic take a breath, and feel His arms around you, because faith hope and love, could never be more true.

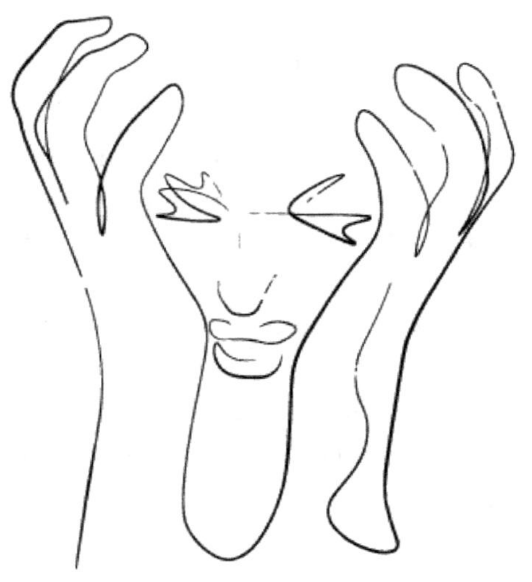

Borrowed Blessings

I often asked myself, whose blessings are we
living, are they ours for the keeping, or
borrowed ones were receiving, who would be so
kind, to give up such a thing, like an angel
helping another, by giving up a wing, how
tremendous this is, if it worked out to be true,
when a voice calls down to me, and says I love
you, so really could it be, a nice gesture from a
friend, to borrow you their blessing, so you get
through till the end, of your life without
struggle, or to be sure you are happy, it would
ensure my hope, to handle Life coming at me,
blessings of all sort, even my own I now borrow,
out to the needy, to help them with their sorrow,
times in their journey, that we all live each day,
look at them with confidence, and say Jesus is
the way, take my hand follow me, don't be
scared of the light, just remember when you
sleep, to pray to me every night.

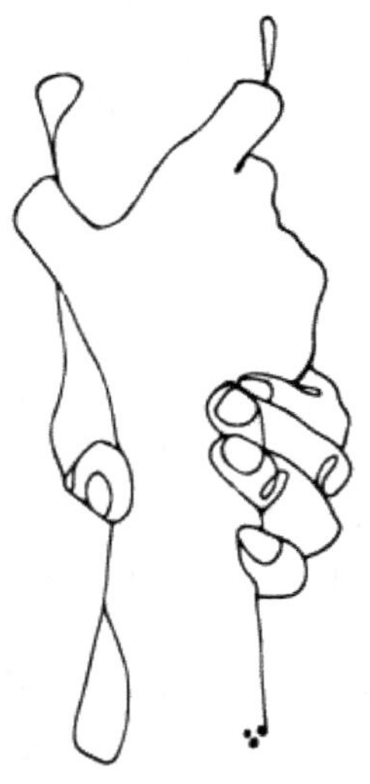

Struggle

The struggle for existence, in this life of mine, some of my busy thoughts, at times aren't so kind, not to anyone alone, but the one in the mirror, why the foggy head at times, why can't I see clearer, when I'm on the loose, when I'm free in person, it seems my choices start to rot, it seems they'll always worsen, as I get older, I'm starting to pray harder, to the man who always listens, he seems to get me farther, in life and my destiny, and the choices on my table, he seems to give me all the things, as Long as I am able, to open up my heart, and accept the lovely gifts, except the fact he hung on the cross, for all of us to live, sin free in our lives, but yet here we sit, thinking of all the reasons, that we always to forget, and ponder all life's choices, and sometimes wonder why, we hear these slamming doors, and then know it's not a lie, well wonder we shall not, because this too shall pass, just keep His love in your heart, and be forever free at last.

Glimmering Prayers

With each new challenge finding life, and learning how to overcome, that Omen of darkness creates a shadow, that only lurks when there is sun, so I line my features with the armor of God, like a seasoned journeyman's prize, I don't let my head hang with shame guilt and pain, and make sure I'm not living in despise, but each day we are blessed, with a gift, yes you and I, it's love that's unconditional, and pure like wine or a clear sky, that highlight all opportunities, of our life that now intertwine, and lead us to new old memories, that we never even set out to find, but lit up like a beacon, with my heart upon my sleeve, I'm pushing to move forward, even if it's slow like the breeze, moving along the morning fog, to make way for light of reassurance, so embrace each breath drawn, we so depend on every occurrence, accompanied with hope, and lots of positive thoughts, and reassure your reflection daily, that it all starts with a simple smile with no fear of ever failing, just perseverance a natural instinct and willingness to lead, and not to be afraid, of the dark skies and what they conceive, but find beauty in the chaos and ride out the storm, and

the bridge Jesus built me, slowly starts to
conform, you see the gold that is priceless, the
wealth is in the spirit, the word of God is a guide
for us, so we don't have to live in fear of it, for a
moment let hearts soften, we all claim to be
tired, when suddenly we are reminded, just why
we are admired, the beauty is the action that we
take in the chance so never let that go, I slowly
let the trust creep back in my heart, for future
blessings I don't know, compassion hope love
and faith, the purity shows in the white tiger, so
be open to the beast that lingers inside, it
represents the inner fighter, act on your morals
and the weight that sins carry and be true
because it is right, because a glimmer of hope is
all it takes, and some prayer to end the night.

www.ingramcontent.com/pod-product-compliance
Lightning Source LLC
LaVergne TN
LVHW010824200726
843508LV00012B/2489

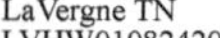